All-New

COOKIE DOUGH FUN

Publications International, Ltd.

Pictured on the front cover: *(clockwise from top left):* Choo-Choo Train *(page 55)*, Brownie Turtle Cookies *(page 10)*, Cookie Tools *(page 64)* and Burger Bliss *(page 92)*.

Pictured on the back cover: *(clockwise from top left):* Sunflower Cookies in Flowerpots *(page 78)*, Color-Bright Ice Cream Sandwiches *(page 20)*, Crayon Cookies *(page 72)* and Peanut Butter Bears *(page 88)*.

ISBN: 1-4127-2135-0

Manufactured in China.

8 7 6 5 4 3 2 1

Microwave Cooking: Microwave ovens vary in wattage. Use the cooking times as guidelines and check for doneness before adding more time.

All-New COOKIE DOUGH FUN

COOKIE DOUGH MANIA

Capture the moment with cookies. Travel through the pages of this whimsical cookbook and discover dozens of magical ways to use cookie dough to make all of your child's cookie fantasies come true. Dazzle your favorite cookie monsters with creative cookie treats or keep their minds and little hands busy for hours exploring their own imaginations with every cookie decoration. It has never been easier to add some fun to brown-bag lunches, after-school snacks and all your children's parties.

General Guidelines

• Measure all the ingredients and assemble them in the order called for in the recipe.

• All cookie dough should be well chilled before using. Unless the recipe states otherwise, work with the recommended portion of dough called for and refrigerate the remaining dough until needed.

• Follow recipe directions and baking times. Check for doneness using the test given in the recipe.

• Most refrigerated cookie dough expands considerably when baked. Always leave two inches between cookies when placing them on cookie sheets.

Supplies:

Some of the recipes in *All-New Cookie Dough Fun* call for special equipment or nonfood items; these are always listed in the recipe under the heading

"Supplies." Most of the supplies listed are available in stores carrying cake decorating equipment and in supermarkets. Additional equipment you may need includes a pastry brush, lollipop sticks, cardboard, pastry bags and decorating tips.

Kitchen Equipment:

Equipment not listed under "Supplies" are items typically found in a well-equipped kitchen: mixing bowls, cookie and baking sheets, rolling pins, saucepans, aluminum foil, waxed paper and cookie cutters.

Special Techniques

Making Patterns:

When a pattern is to be used only once, as for the Choo-Choo Train (page 55), make the pattern out of waxed paper. Using the diagram(s) and photo as guides, draw the pattern pieces on waxed paper. Cut the pieces out and place them on the cookie. Cut around the pattern pieces with a sharp knife. Remove the pattern pieces and discard. Continue as directed in the recipe.

For patterns that are used more than once, make the pattern more durable by using clean, lightweight cardboard or poster board. Using the diagram(s) and photo as guides, draw the pattern pieces on the cardboard. Cut the pieces out and lightly spray one side with nonstick cooking spray. Place pattern pieces, sprayed side down, on the rolled-out dough and cut around them with a sharp knife. Reuse the pattern pieces to make as many cutouts as needed.

Tinting Coconut:

Dilute a few drops of food coloring with ½ teaspoon water in a large plastic food storage bag. Add 1 to 1⅓ cups flaked coconut. Close the bag and shake well until the coconut is evenly coated. If a deeper color is desired, add more diluted food coloring and shake again.

Be Creative

Let your imagination go wild— decorate your way! Use the decorations, suggestions and photos as a starting point to set you on your way. Let your creative flair show. Feel free to change colors or shapes to suit your family or party. The White Decorator Frosting (page 48) can always be used instead of purchased frosting; simply tint it to create all the shades you desire. Most importantly— have fun!

5

CHILD'S PLAY

Cheery Chocolate Animal Cookies

What you need:

- 1 (10-ounce) package REESE'S® Peanut Butter Chips
- 1 cup HERSHEY'S Semi-Sweet Chocolate Chips
- 2 tablespoons shortening *(do not use butter, margarine or oil)*
- 1 package (20 ounces) chocolate sandwich cookies
- 1 package (10 ounces) animal crackers

1. Line trays or cookie sheets with waxed paper.

2. In 2-quart glass measuring cup with handle, combine chips and shortening. Microwave on HIGH (100% power) 1½ to 2 minutes or until chips are melted and mixture is smooth when stirred.

3. With fork, dip each cookie into melted chip mixture; gently tap fork on side of cup to remove excess chocolate. Place chocolate-coated cookies on prepared trays; top each cookie with an animal cracker. Chill until chocolate is set, about 30 minutes. Store in airtight container in a cool, dry place.
Makes about 4 dozen cookies

Cheery Chocolate Animal Cookies

Caramel Marshmallow Bars

What you need:

CRUMB MIXTURE
1¼ cups all-purpose flour
½ cup sugar
½ cup butter, softened
¼ cup graham cracker
   crumbs
¼ teaspoon salt
½ cup chopped salted
   peanuts

FILLING
¾ cup caramel ice cream
   topping
½ cup salted peanuts
½ cup miniature
   marshmallows
½ cup milk chocolate chips

1 Preheat oven to 350°F.
Grease and flour 9-inch
square baking pan.

2 For crumb mixture,
combine flour, sugar,
butter, graham cracker crumbs
and salt in small bowl. Beat at
low speed of electric mixer,
scraping bowl often, 1 to 2
minutes or until mixture is
crumbly. Stir in ½ cup chopped
peanuts. Reserve ¾ cup crumb
mixture. Press remaining crumb
mixture onto bottom of
prepared pan.

3 Bake 10 to 12 minutes or
until lightly browned.

4 For filling, spread caramel
topping evenly over hot
crust. Sprinkle with ½ cup
peanuts, marshmallows and
chocolate chips. Sprinkle ¾ cup
reserved crumb mixture over
chocolate chips.

5 Continue baking
10 to 12 minutes or until
marshmallows just start to
brown. Cool on wire rack about
30 minutes. Cover; refrigerate
1 to 2 hours or until firm. Cut
into bars. *Makes about
2½ dozen bars*

Tip: *For an extra special treat,
serve these kid-pleasing
bars with a scoop of ice cream.*

Brownie Turtle Cookies

What you need:

- 2 squares (1 ounce each) unsweetened baking chocolate
- 1/3 cup solid vegetable shortening
- 1 cup granulated sugar
- 1/2 teaspoon vanilla extract
- 2 large eggs
- 1 1/4 cups all-purpose flour
- 1/2 teaspoon baking powder
- 1/2 teaspoon salt
- 1 cup "M&M's"® Milk Chocolate Mini Baking Bits, divided
- 1 cup pecan halves
- 1/3 cup caramel ice cream topping
- 1/3 cup shredded coconut
- 1/3 cup finely chopped pecans

1 Preheat oven to 350°F. Lightly grease cookie sheets; set aside.

2 Heat chocolate and shortening in 2-quart saucepan over low heat, stirring constantly until melted; remove from heat. Mix in sugar, vanilla and eggs. Blend in flour, baking powder and salt. Stir in 2/3 cup *"M&M's"® Milk Chocolate Mini Baking Bits.*

3 For each cookie, arrange 3 pecan halves, with ends almost touching at center, on prepared cookie sheets. Drop dough by rounded teaspoonfuls onto center of each group of pecans; mound the dough slightly.

4 Bake 8 to 10 minutes just until set. Do not overbake. Cool completely on wire racks.

5 In small bowl combine ice cream topping, coconut and nuts; top each cookie with about 1 1/2 teaspoons mixture. Press remaining *1/3 cup "M&M's"® Milk Chocolate Mini Baking Bits* into topping.

Makes about 2 1/2 dozen cookies

Hershey's Milk Chocolate Chip Giant Cookies

What you need:

6 tablespoons butter, softened
½ cup granulated sugar
¼ cup packed light brown sugar
½ teaspoon vanilla extract
1 egg
1 cup all-purpose flour
½ teaspoon baking soda
2 cups (11.5-ounce package) HERSHEY'S Milk Chocolate Chips
Frosting (optional)
Ice cream (optional)

1 Heat oven to 350°F. Line two 9-inch round baking pans with foil, extending foil over edges of pans.

2 Beat butter, granulated sugar, brown sugar and vanilla until fluffy. Add egg; beat well. Stir together flour and baking soda; gradually add to butter mixture, beating until well blended. Stir in milk chocolate chips.

3 Spread one half of batter into each prepared pan, spreading to 1 inch from edge. (Cookies will spread to edge when baking.)

4 Bake 18 to 22 minutes or until lightly browned. Cool completely; carefully lift cookies from pans and remove foil. Frost, if desired. Cut each cookie into wedges; serve topped with scoop of ice cream, if desired.

Makes about 12 to 16 servings

Tip: Bake cookies on the middle rack of the oven, one pan at a time. Uneven browning can occur if baking on more than one rack at the same time.

Hershey's Milk Chocolate Chip Giant Cookie

Fudgey German Chocolate Sandwich Cookies

What you need:

1¾ cups all-purpose flour
1½ cups sugar
 ¾ cup (1½ sticks) butter or
    margarine, softened
 ⅔ cup HERSHEY'S Cocoa
    or HERSHEY'S Dutch
    Processed Cocoa
 ¾ teaspoon baking soda
 ¼ teaspoon salt
 2 eggs
 2 tablespoons milk
 1 teaspoon vanilla extract
 ½ cup finely chopped
    pecans
    Coconut and Pecan Filling
    (recipe follows)

1 Heat oven to 350°F.

2 Stir together flour, sugar, butter, cocoa, baking soda and salt in large bowl. Add eggs, milk and vanilla; beat at medium speed of electric mixer until blended. Dough will be stiff. Stir in pecans.

3 Form dough into 1¼-inch balls. Place on ungreased cookie sheet; flatten slightly.

4 Bake 9 to 11 minutes or until almost set. Cool slightly; remove from cookie sheet to wire rack. Cool completely. Prepare Coconut and Pecan Filling. Put cookies together in pairs with about 1 heaping tablespoon filling for each sandwich. Serve warm or at room temperature.

*Makes about
17 sandwich cookies*

Coconut and Pecan Filling

 ½ cup (1 stick) butter or
    margarine
 ½ cup packed light brown
    sugar
 ¼ cup light corn syrup
 1 cup MOUNDS® Sweetened
    Coconut Flakes, toasted
 1 cup finely chopped
    pecans
 1 teaspoon vanilla extract

1 Melt butter in medium saucepan over medium heat; add brown sugar and corn syrup. Stir constantly until thick and bubbly. Remove from heat; stir in coconut, pecans and vanilla. Use warm.

*Makes about
2 cups filling*

*Fudgey German Chocolate
Sandwich Cookies*

Child's Play

Kids' Favorite Jumbo Chippers

What you need:

1 cup (2 sticks) butter, softened
¾ cup granulated sugar
¾ cup packed brown sugar
2 eggs
1 teaspoon vanilla
2¼ cups all-purpose flour
1 teaspoon baking soda
¾ teaspoon salt
1 package (9 ounces) candy-coated chocolate pieces
1 cup peanut butter-flavored chips

1 Preheat oven to 375°F.

2 Beat butter, granulated sugar and brown sugar in large bowl until light and fluffy. Beat in eggs and vanilla. Add flour, baking soda and salt. Beat until well blended. Stir in chocolate pieces and peanut butter chips. Drop by rounded tablespoonfuls 3 inches apart onto ungreased cookie sheets.

3 Bake 10 to 12 minutes or until edges are golden brown. Let cookies stand on cookie sheets 2 minutes. Remove cookies to wire racks; cool completely.

Makes 3 dozen cookies

Tip: *For a change of pace, substitute white chocolate chips, chocolate chips, chocolate-covered raisins, toffee bits or any of your cookie monsters' favorite candy pieces for the candy-coated chocolate pieces.*

Chocolate Peanut Butter Cup Cookies

What you need:

COOKIES
- 1 cup semisweet chocolate chips
- 2 squares (1 ounce each) unsweetened baking chocolate
- 1 cup sugar
- ½ Butter Flavor CRISCO® Stick or ½ cup Butter Flavor CRISCO® all-vegetable shortening
- 2 eggs
- 1 teaspoon salt
- 1 teaspoon vanilla
- 1½ cups plus 2 tablespoons all-purpose flour
- ½ teaspoon baking soda
- ¾ cup finely chopped peanuts
- 36 miniature peanut butter cups, unwrapped

DRIZZLE
- 1 cup peanut butter chips

*Butter Flavor Crisco is artificially flavored.

1 Heat oven to 350°F. Place sheets of foil on countertop for cooling cookies.

2 For cookies, combine chocolate chips and chocolate squares in microwave-safe measuring cup or bowl. Microwave at 50% power (MEDIUM). Stir after 2 minutes. Repeat until smooth (or melt on rangetop in small saucepan over very low heat). Cool slightly.

3 Combine sugar and ½ cup shortening in large bowl. Beat at medium speed of electric mixer until blended and crumbly. Beat in eggs, one at a time, then salt and vanilla. Reduce speed to low. Add chocolate slowly. Mix until well blended. Stir in flour and baking soda with spoon until well blended. Shape dough into 1¼-inch balls. Roll in nuts. Place 2 inches apart on ungreased baking sheet.

4 Bake at 350°F for 8 to 10 minutes or until set. *Do not overbake.* Press peanut butter cup into center of each cookie immediately. Cool 2 minutes on baking sheet. Remove cookies to foil to cool completely.

5 For drizzle, place peanut butter chips in heavy resealable sandwich bag. Seal. Microwave at 50% power (MEDIUM). Knead bag after 1 minute. Repeat until smooth (or melt by placing bag in hot water). Cut tiny tip off corner of bag. Squeeze out and drizzle over cookies.

Makes 3 dozen cookies

Chocolate Peanut Butter Cup Cookies

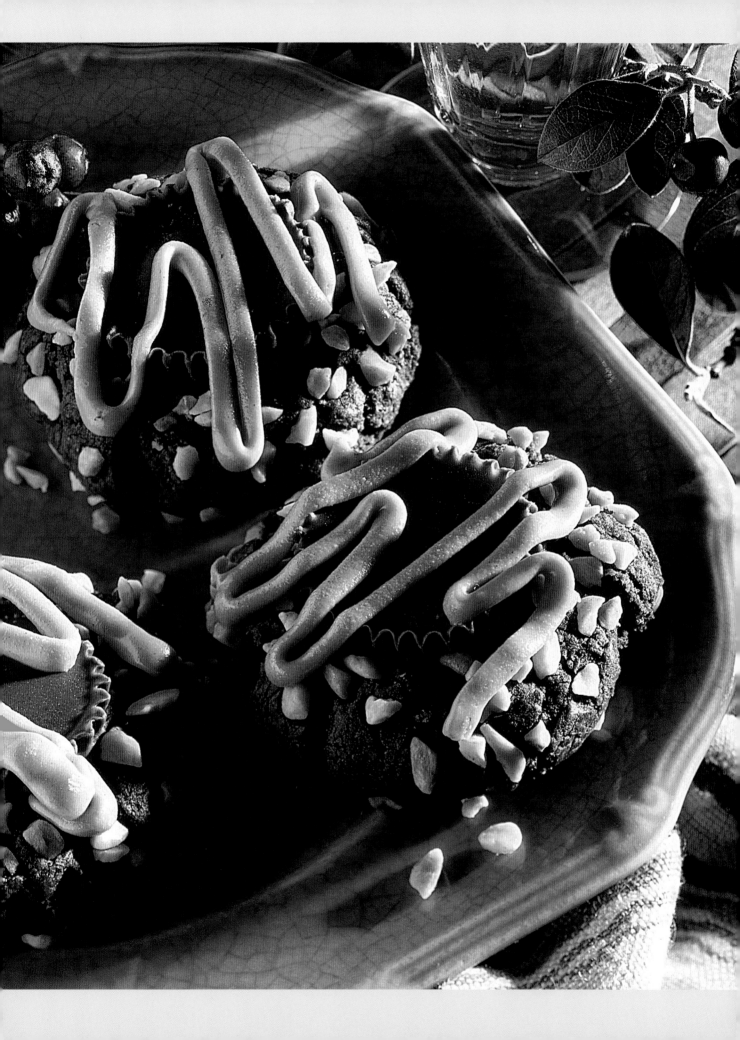

Color-Bright Ice Cream Sandwiches

What you need:

¾ cup (1½ sticks) butter or
   margarine, softened
¾ cup creamy peanut butter
1¼ cups firmly packed light
   brown sugar
1 large egg
1 teaspoon vanilla extract
1½ cups all-purpose flour
1 teaspoon baking soda
¼ teaspoon salt
1¾ cups "M&M's"® Chocolate
   Mini Baking Bits, divided
2 quarts vanilla or chocolate
   ice cream, slightly
   softened

1 Preheat oven to 350°F.

2 In large bowl cream butter, peanut butter and sugar until light and fluffy; beat in egg and vanilla.

3 In medium bowl combine flour, baking soda and salt; blend into creamed mixture. Stir in *1⅓ cups "M&M's"® Chocolate Mini Baking Bits.*

4 Shape dough into 1¼-inch balls. Place about 2 inches apart on ungreased cookie sheets. Gently flatten to about ½-inch thickness with fingertips. Place 7 or 8 of the remaining *"M&M's"® Chocolate Mini Baking Bits* on each cookie; press in lightly.

5 Bake 10 to 12 minutes or until edges are light brown. *Do not overbake.* Cool about 1 minute on cookie sheets; cool completely on wire racks. Assemble cookies in pairs with about ⅓ cup ice cream; press cookies together lightly. Wrap each sandwich in plastic wrap; freeze until firm.
Makes about 24 ice cream sandwiches

Color-Bright Ice Cream Sandwiches

Marvelous Cookie Bars

What you need:

½ cup (1 stick) butter or margarine, softened
1 cup firmly packed light brown sugar
2 large eggs
1⅓ cups all-purpose flour
1 cup quick-cooking or old-fashioned oats, uncooked
⅓ cup unsweetened cocoa powder
1 teaspoon baking powder
½ teaspoon salt
¼ teaspoon baking soda
½ cup chopped walnuts, divided
1 cup "M&M's"® Semi-Sweet Chocolate Mini Baking Bits, divided
½ cup cherry preserves
¼ cup shredded coconut

1 Preheat oven to 350°F. Lightly grease 9×9×2-inch baking pan; set aside.

2 In large bowl cream butter and sugar until light and fluffy; beat in eggs.

3 In medium bowl combine flour, oats, cocoa powder, baking powder, salt and baking soda; blend into creamed mixture. Stir in ¼ *cup nuts* and ¾ *cup "M&M's"® Semi-Sweet Chocolate Mini Baking Bits.* Reserve 1 cup dough; spread remaining dough into prepared pan.

4 Combine preserves, coconut and remaining ¼ cup nuts; spread evenly over dough to within ½ inch of edge. Drop reserved dough by rounded teaspoonfuls over preserves mixture; sprinkle with remaining ¼ *cup "M&M's"® Semi-Sweet Chocolate Mini Baking Bits.*

5 Bake 25 to 30 minutes or until slightly firm near edges. Cool completely. Cut into bars. Store in tightly covered container.

Makes 16 bars

Cookie Decorating Party

1 container (16 ounces) strawberry frosting, at room temperature
48 vanilla wafers or sugar cookies
¼ to ½ pound assorted Valentine candies, such as cinnamon hearts, conversation hearts, chocolate candies, red hots and heart-shaped sprinkles

1 Stir frosting in container until soft and creamy. Divide frosting evenly among small paper cups to equal one paper cup per child.

2 Give each child an equal number of cookies, one paper cup of frosting and assortment of candies. Have children dip cookies into frosting or spread frosting with backs of spoons. Decorate with candies or sprinkles as desired.
Makes 4 dozen cookies

Tip: *Use your imagination and create your own decorating party. These cookies are perfect for all holiday and birthday parties. Use different colored frostings, holiday candies and fun sprinkles to create themed cookies for every occasion.*

Old-Fashioned Ice Cream Sandwiches

2 squares (1 ounce each) semisweet baking chocolate, coarsely chopped
½ cup butter, softened
½ cup sugar
1 egg
1 teaspoon vanilla
1½ cups all-purpose flour
¼ teaspoon baking soda
¼ teaspoon salt
Softened vanilla or mint chocolate chip ice cream*

*One quart of ice cream can be softened in the microwave at HIGH about 20 seconds.

1 Place chocolate in 1-cup glass measuring cup. Microwave, uncovered, at HIGH 1 to 1½ minutes or until chocolate is melted, stirring after 1 minute; set aside.

2 Beat butter and sugar in large bowl until light and fluffy. Beat in egg and vanilla. Gradually beat in chocolate. Combine flour, baking soda and salt in small bowl; add to butter mixture. Form dough into two discs; wrap in plastic wrap and refrigerate until firm, at least 2 hours or up to 3 days.

3 Preheat oven to 350°F. Grease cookie sheets.

4 Roll one dough disc between two sheets of waxed paper to ¼- to ⅛-inch thickness. Remove top sheet of waxed paper; invert dough onto prepared cookie sheet. Score dough into 3×2-inch rectangles. *Do not cut completely through dough.* Cut excess scraps of dough from edges; add to second disc of dough and repeat rolling and scoring until all of dough is scored. Pierce each rectangle with fork.

5 Bake 10 minutes or until set. Let cookies stand on cookie sheets 1 minute. Cut through score marks while cookies are still warm. Remove cookies to wire racks; cool completely. Spread half of cookies with softened ice cream; top with remaining cookies. Wrap in plastic wrap and freeze 1 hour or up to 2 days. *Makes about 8 ice cream sandwiches*

Old-Fashioned Ice Cream Sandwiches

Chocolate Crackletops

What you need:

2 cups all-purpose flour
2 teaspoons baking powder
2 cups granulated sugar
½ cup (1 stick) butter or
　　margarine
4 squares (1 ounce each)
　　unsweetened baking
　　chocolate, chopped
4 large eggs, lightly beaten
2 teaspoons vanilla extract
1¾ cups "M&M's"® Chocolate
　　Mini Baking Bits
　　Additional granulated
　　sugar

1 Combine flour and baking powder; set aside.

2 In 2-quart saucepan over medium heat combine 2 cups sugar, butter and chocolate, stirring until butter and chocolate are melted; remove from heat. Gradually stir in eggs and vanilla. Stir in flour mixture until well blended. Chill mixture 1 hour. Stir in "M&M's"® Chocolate Mini Baking Bits; chill mixture an additional 1 hour.

3 Preheat oven to 350°F. Line cookie sheets with foil.

4 With sugar-dusted hands, roll dough into 1-inch balls; roll balls in additional granulated sugar. Place about 2 inches apart onto prepared cookie sheets.

5 Bake 10 to 12 minutes. Do not overbake. Cool completely on wire racks. Store in tightly covered container.

*Makes about
5 dozen cookies*

Tip: *Make your kids smile from ear to ear when they find these perfectly packable cookies in their lunch boxes.*

Peanut Butter Chips and Jelly Bars

What you need:

1½ cups all-purpose flour
½ cup sugar
¾ teaspoon baking powder
½ cup (1 stick) cold butter or
    margarine
1 egg, beaten
¾ cup grape jelly
1⅔ cups (10-ounce package)
    REESE'S® Peanut Butter
    Chips, divided

1 Heat oven to 375°F.
Grease 9-inch square
baking pan.

2 Stir together flour, sugar
and baking powder in
large bowl. With pastry blender
or two knives, cut in butter until
mixture resembles coarse
crumbs. Add egg; blend well.
Reserve 1 cup mixture; press
remaining mixture onto bottom
of prepared pan. Stir jelly to
soften; spread evenly over
crust. Sprinkle 1 cup peanut
butter chips over jelly. Stir
together reserved crumb
mixture with remaining ⅔ cup
chips; sprinkle over top.

3 Bake 25 to 30 minutes or
until lightly browned. Cool
completely in pan on wire rack.
Cut into bars.

Makes about 16 bars

Tip: *For a whimsical twist on
this tried-and-true classic,
use cookie cutters to cut out shapes
for added fun.*

*Peanut Butter Chips
and Jelly Bars*

Marshmallow Sandwich Cookies

What you need:

1¼ cups sugar
⅔ cup butter
¼ cup light corn syrup
1 egg
1 teaspoon vanilla
2 cups all-purpose flour
½ cup unsweetened cocoa powder
2 teaspoons baking soda
¼ teaspoon salt
Additional sugar for rolling
24 large marshmallows

1 Preheat oven to 350°F.

2 Beat 1¼ cups sugar and butter in large bowl until light and fluffy. Beat in corn syrup, egg and vanilla. Combine flour, cocoa, baking soda and salt in medium bowl; add to butter mixture. Beat until well blended. Cover and refrigerate dough 15 minutes or until firm enough to roll into balls.

3 Place sugar in shallow dish. Roll tablespoonfuls of dough into 1-inch balls; roll in sugar to coat. Place cookies 3 inches apart on ungreased cookie sheets.

4 Bake 10 to 11 minutes or until set. Remove cookies to wire racks; cool completely.

5 To assemble sandwiches, place one marshmallow on flat side of one cookie on paper plate. Microwave at HIGH 12 seconds or until marshmallow is softened. Immediately place another cookie, flat side down, on top of hot marshmallow; press together slightly. Repeat with remaining cookies and marshmallows.

Makes about 2 dozen sandwich cookies

Chocolate Surprise Cookies

2¾ cups all-purpose flour
 ¾ cup unsweetened cocoa
 powder
½ teaspoon baking powder
½ teaspoon baking soda
 1 cup (2 sticks) butter,
 softened
1½ cups packed light brown
 sugar
 ½ cup plus 1 tablespoon
 granulated sugar,
 divided
 2 eggs
 1 teaspoon vanilla
 1 cup chopped pecans,
 divided
 1 package (9 ounces)
 caramels coated in milk
 chocolate
 3 squares (1 ounce each)
 white chocolate,
 coarsely chopped

1 Preheat oven to 375°F.

2 Combine flour, cocoa, baking powder and baking soda in medium bowl; set aside.

3 Beat butter, brown sugar and ½ cup granulated sugar with electric mixer at medium speed until light and fluffy; beat in eggs and vanilla.

Gradually add flour mixture and ½ cup pecans; beat well. Cover dough; refrigerate 15 minutes or until firm enough to roll into balls.

4 Place remaining ½ cup pecans and 1 tablespoon granulated sugar in shallow dish. Roll tablespoonful of dough around 1 caramel candy, covering completely; press one side into nut mixture. Place, nut side up, on ungreased cookie sheet. Repeat with additional dough and candies, placing cookies 3 inches apart.

5 Bake 10 to 12 minutes or until set and slightly cracked. Let stand on cookie sheet 2 minutes. Transfer cookies to wire rack; cool completely.

6 Place white chocolate pieces in small resealable plastic freezer bag; seal bag. Microwave at MEDIUM (50% power) 2 minutes. Turn bag over; microwave 2 to 3 minutes or until melted. Knead bag until chocolate is smooth. Cut off tiny corner of bag; drizzle chocolate onto cookies. Let stand about 30 minutes or until chocolate is set.

*Makes about
3½ dozen cookies*

COOKIE DOUGH ART

Mini Pizza Cookies

What you need:

1 (20-ounce) tube of
  refrigerated sugar
  cookie dough
2 cups (16 ounces) prepared
  pink frosting
  "M&M's"® Chocolate Mini
  Baking Bits
  Variety of additional
  toppings such as
  shredded coconut,
  granola, raisins, nuts,
  small pretzels, snack
  mixes, sunflower seeds,
  popped corn and mini
  marshmallows

1 Preheat oven to 350°F.
Lightly grease cookie
sheets; set aside.

2 Divide dough into 8 equal
portions. On lightly floured
surface, roll each portion of
dough into ¼-inch-thick circle;
place about 2 inches apart onto
prepared cookie sheets.

3 Bake 10 to 13 minutes
or until golden brown on
edges. Cool completely on
wire racks. Spread top of each
pizza with frosting; sprinkle with
"M&M's"® Chocolate Mini Baking
Bits and 2 or 3 suggested
toppings.   *Makes 8 cookies*

36

Mini Pizza Cookies

Musical Instrument Cookies

1 package (about 18 ounces) refrigerated sugar cookie dough
All-purpose flour (optional)

DECORATIONS

Assorted colored frostings, colored gels, colored sugars, candy and small decors

1 Preheat oven to 350°F. Grease cookie sheets.

2 Remove dough from wrapper according to package directions. Divide dough into 2 equal sections. Reserve 1 section; cover and refrigerate remaining section.

3 Roll reserved dough on lightly floured surface to ¼-inch thickness. Sprinkle with flour to minimize sticking, if necessary. Cut out cookies using about 3½-inch musical note and instrument cookie cutters. Place cookies 2 inches apart on prepared cookie sheets. Repeat with remaining dough.

4 Bake 10 to 12 minutes or until edges are lightly browned. Remove from oven. Let cool on cookie sheets 2 minutes. Remove to wire racks; cool completely.

5 Decorate with colored frostings, gels, sugars and assorted decors as shown in photo. *Makes about 2 dozen cookies*

Tip: If you do not have cookie cuters, create a pattern using the directions on page 5.

Chocolate Mint Ravioli Cookies

What you need:

1 package (15 ounces) refrigerated pie crusts
1 bar (7 ounces) cookies 'n' mint chocolate candy
1 egg
1 tablespoon water
Powdered sugar

1 Preheat oven to 400°F.

2 Unfold 1 pie crust on lightly floured surface. Roll into 13-inch circle. Cut pastry into 24 circles with 2½-inch round cookie cutter, rerolling scraps if necessary. Repeat with remaining pie crust.

3 Separate candy bar into pieces marked on bar. Cut each chocolate piece in half. Beat egg and water together in small bowl with fork. Brush half of pastry circles lightly with egg mixture. Place 1 piece of chocolate in center of each circle. (There will be some candy bar left over.) Top with remaining pastry circles. Seal edges with tines of fork.

4 Place on ungreased cookie sheets. Brush with egg mixture.

5 Bake 8 to 10 minutes or until golden brown. Remove from cookie sheets; cool completely on wire racks. Dust with powdered sugar.
Makes 2 dozen cookies

Tip: Mix it up! Substitute your favorite candy bar for the cookies 'n' mint chocolate candy for a completely different taste.

Chocolate Mint Ravioli Cookies

Cookie Dough Art

Playing Card Cookies

What you need:

**1 package (about
    18 ounces) refrigerated
    sugar cookie dough
All-purpose flour
    (optional)**

**DECORATIONS
    Cookie Glaze (recipe
        follows)
    Assorted colored icings**

1 Preheat oven to 350°F.
Grease cookie sheets.

2 Remove dough from
wrapper according to
package directions. Divide
dough into 2 equal sections.
Reserve 1 section; cover and
refrigerate remaining section.

3 Roll reserved section on
lightly floured surface to
¼-inch thickness. Sprinkle with
flour to minimize sticking, if
necessary. Cut out 3½×2½-inch
rectangles with sharp knife.
Place cookies 2 inches apart on
prepared cookie sheets. Repeat
steps with remaining dough.

4 Bake 8 to 10 minutes or
until edges are lightly
browned. Remove from oven
and straighten cookie edges
with spatula. Cool on cookie
sheets 2 minutes. Remove to
wire racks; cool completely.

5 Place cookies on wire
racks set over waxed
paper. Spread Cookie Glaze
over cookies. Let stand at room
temperature 40 minutes or
until glaze is set. Pipe colored
icings onto cookies to resemble
various playing card designs.
*Makes about
26 cookies*

Cookie Glaze

**4 cups powdered sugar
4 to 6 tablespoons milk**

1 Combine powdered sugar
and enough milk, one
tablespoon at a time, to make
a medium-thick pourable glaze.

Our House

What you need:

**1 package (about
18 ounces) refrigerated
cookie dough, any flavor
All-purpose flour
(optional)**

DECORATIONS

**Blue, green, white
and purple icings,
granulated sugar,
yellow-colored sugar,
green gumdrops, red
licorice, small decors
and hard candies**

1 Preheat oven to 350°F.
Line large cookie sheet
with parchment paper.

2 Remove dough from
wrapper according to
package directions. Roll small
piece of dough into 1½-inch
square; reserve.

3 Press remaining dough
into 12×9-inch rectangle
on prepared cookie sheet.
Sprinkle with flour to minimize
sticking, if necessary.

4 Place reserved dough at
top of rectangle to make
chimney. Press to seal.

5 Bake 10 to 12 minutes
or until edges are lightly
browned. Cool on baking sheet
5 minutes. Slide house and
parchment paper onto wire
rack; cool completely.

6 Decorate as shown in
photo. Use flat decorating
tip for clapboards and shingles,
yellow colored sugar for
windows, star decorating tip
for columns and steps, and
gumdrops for bushes.
Makes 1 cookie house

Tip: *This is a perfect rainy–day
project. Keep your kids
entertained by decorating this cookie
house as directed or let their minds
go wild and decorate it however they
like.*

Peanut Butter and Jelly Sandwich Cookies

What you need:

1 package (about 18 ounces) refrigerated sugar cookie dough
1 tablespoon unsweetened cocoa powder
All-purpose flour (optional)

FILLINGS
1¾ cups creamy peanut butter
½ cup grape jam or jelly

1 Remove dough from wrapper according to package directions. Reserve ¼ section of dough; cover and refrigerate remaining ¾ section of dough. Combine reserved dough and cocoa in small bowl; refrigerate.

2 Shape remaining ¾ section of dough into 5½-inch log. Sprinkle with flour to minimize sticking, if necessary. Remove chocolate dough from refrigerator; roll on sheet of waxed paper to 9½×6½-inch rectangle. Place dough log in center of rectangle.

3 Bring chocolate dough and waxed paper edges up and together over log. Press gently on top and sides of dough so entire log is wrapped in chocolate dough. Flatten log slightly to form square. Wrap in waxed paper. Freeze 10 minutes.

4 Preheat oven to 350°F.

5 Remove waxed paper. Cut log into ¼-inch slices. Place slices 2 inches apart on ungreased cookie sheets. Reshape dough edges to form a square, if necessary. Press dough slightly to form indentations so dough resembles slice of bread.

6 Bake 8 to 11 minutes or until lightly browned. Remove from oven and straighten cookie edges with spatula. Cool 2 minutes on cookie sheets. Remove to wire racks; cool completely.

7 To make sandwich, spread about 1 tablespoon peanut butter on underside of 1 cookie. Spread about ½ tablespoon jam over peanut butter; top with second cookie, pressing gently. Repeat with remaining cookies.
Makes 11 sandwich cookies

Peanut Butter and Jelly Sandwich Cookies

Kitty Cookies

**1 package (about
  18 ounces) refrigerated
  sugar cookie dough or
  desired flavor
All-purpose flour
  (optional)**

DECORATIONS

**White Decorator Frosting
  (recipe follows)
Assorted colored icings,
  colored candies and red
  licorice**

1 Preheat oven to 350°F.

2 Remove dough from
wrapper according to
package directions. Divide
dough into 2 equal sections.
Reserve 1 section; cover and
refrigerate remaining section.

3 Roll reserved dough on
lightly floured surface to
⅛-inch thickness. Sprinkle with
flour to minimize sticking, if
necessary.

4 Cut out cookies using
3½-inch kitty face cookie
cutter or pattern (see page 5).
Place cookies 2 inches apart
on ungreased cookie sheets.
Repeat with remaining dough.

5 Bake 8 to 10 minutes or
until firm but not browned.
Let cool on cookie sheets
2 minutes. Remove to wire
racks; cool completely.

6 Decorate with white
and colored icings and
candies as shown in photo.

*Makes about
20 cookies*

White Decorator Frosting

**4 cups powdered sugar
½ cup vegetable shortening
  or unsalted butter
1 tablespoon corn syrup
6 to 8 tablespoons milk
Assorted paste food
  colorings**

1 Beat sugar, shortening,
corn syrup and milk in
medium bowl at high speed of
electric mixer 2 minutes or until
fluffy. Add food colorings to
achieve desired colors.

Under the Sea

**1 package (about
   18 ounces) refrigerated
   sugar cookie dough
Blue liquid or paste food
   coloring
All-purpose flour
   (optional)**

DECORATIONS
**Blue Royal Icing (recipe
   follows)
Assorted small decors,
   gummy candies and
   hard candies**

1 Preheat oven to 350°F.
Grease 12-inch pizza pan.

2 Remove dough from
wrapper according to
package directions. Combine
dough and blue food coloring,
a few drops at a time, in large
bowl until desired color is
achieved; blend until smooth.

3 Press dough into bottom
of prepared pan, leaving
about ¾-inch space between
edge of dough and pan.
Sprinkle dough with flour to
minimize sticking, if necessary.

4 Bake 10 to 12 minutes or
until set in center. Cool
completely in pan on wire rack.

Run spatula between cookie
crust and pan after 10 to 15
minutes to loosen.

5 Pipe or spread Blue
Royal Icing randomly over
cookie to resemble texture of
sea. Once icing is set, decorate
with decors and candies as
shown in photo.
Makes 10 to 12 wedges

Blue Royal Icing

**1 egg white,* at room
   temperature
2 to 2½ cups sifted
   powdered sugar
½ teaspoon almond extract
   Blue liquid or paste food
   coloring**

*Use clean, uncracked egg.

1 Beat egg white in small
bowl at high speed of
electric mixer until foamy.

2 Gradually add 2 cups
powdered sugar and
almond extract. Beat at low
speed until moistened. Increase
mixer speed to high and beat
until icing is stiff, adding
additional powdered sugar
if needed. Tint icing blue with
food coloring, a few drops at a
time, until desired color is
achieved.

Dude Ranch

1 package (about
18 ounces) refrigerated
sugar cookie dough
All-purpose flour
(optional)

DECORATIONS

Royal Icing (page 54)
Assorted food colorings,
fruit chews, small
decors and hard candies
12 (4×3-inch) frosted
chocolate toaster
pastries
35 (7½-inch) pretzel rods

SUPPLIES

Cardboard, decorative
paper and plastic wrap

1 Draw patterns for cowboys and horses on cardboard using diagrams on page 54; cut out patterns.

2 Preheat oven to 350°F. Grease cookie sheets.

3 Remove dough from wrapper according to package directions. Divide dough into 2 equal sections. Reserve 1 section; cover and refrigerate remaining section.

4 Roll reserved dough on lightly floured surface to ¼-inch thickness. Sprinkle with flour to minimize sticking, if necessary. Lay sheet of waxed paper over dough. Place patterns over waxed paper. Cut dough around patterns with sharp knife; remove patterns and waxed paper. Place cookies 2 inches apart on prepared cookie sheets. Repeat with remaining dough.

5 Bake 10 to 12 minutes or until edges are lightly browned. Remove from oven. Let cool on cookie sheets 2 minutes. Remove to wire racks; cool completely.

6 Prepare Royal Icing. Tint about 1 cup icing to match color of toaster pastries used for corral floor. Tint small amounts of remaining icing with desired food colors to decorate cowboys and horses; place in small resealable plastic food storage bags. Cut off small corners of bags for piping.

7 Decorate cowboys and horses with colored sugars, decors and hard candies as shown in photo.

continued on page 54

Dude Ranch, continued

8 Cover 20×12-inch piece of cardboard with decorative paper and plastic wrap. Assemble corral floor by placing cardboard with 12-inch side facing you. Pipe icing on bottom of toaster pastries; place vertically, 4 down and 3 across, in center of cardboard.

9 Assemble fence by carefully cutting 5 pretzel rods into 3 equal sections with serrated knife. Pipe icing down 1 whole pretzel rod and 1 cut pretzel rod. Place end to end to fit 12-inch side of corral. Repeat at other 12-inch side. Pipe icing down 1 cut pretzel rod and 2 whole pretzel rods. Place end to end to fit 20-inch side of corral. Pipe icing down 2 whole rods. Place at other 20-inch side, leaving opening for entrance. Continue building fence with 4 additional layers on each side. Let dry. Pipe icing on feet of cowboys and horses; arrange so they can be supported by fence or each other. *Makes 1 fence and 16 cookies*

Royal Icing

2 egg whites*
4 to 4½ cups sifted powdered sugar
1 teaspoon almond extract

*Use clean, uncracked eggs.

1 Beat egg whites in medium bowl at high speed of electric mixer until foamy.

2 Gradually add 4 cups powdered sugar and almond extract. Beat at low speed until moistened. Increase mixer speed to high and beat until icing is stiff, adding additional powdered sugar if needed.

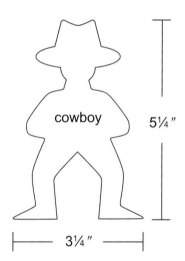

cowboy   5¼ "

3¼ "

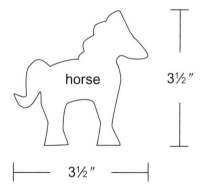

horse   3½ "

3½ "

Choo-Choo Train

What you need:

**1 package (about
18 ounces) refrigerated
peanut butter cookie
dough or desired flavor
All-purpose flour
(optional)**

DECORATIONS
**Blue Cookie Glaze
(page 56)
Assorted colored icings,
colored candies, small
decors and 2 small
peanut butter sandwich
crackers**

SUPPLIES
Cardboard

1 Draw patterns for 4 train cars on cardboard, using diagrams on page 56; cut out patterns.

2 Preheat oven to 350°F. Line cookie sheets with parchment paper.

3 Remove dough from wrapper according to package directions. Roll dough on lightly floured surface to 18×13-inch rectangle. Sprinkle with flour to minimize sticking, if necessary. Place on prepared cookie sheet.

4 Bake 8 to 10 minutes or until lightly browned. Cool on baking sheet 5 minutes. Slide cookie and parchment paper onto wire rack; cool 5 minutes.

5 While still warm, lay sheet of waxed paper over cookie. Place patterns over waxed paper. Cut cookie around patterns with sharp knife; remove patterns and waxed paper. Cover with towel; cool completely.

6 Spread Blue Cookie Glaze on train cars as shown in photo. Allow glaze to set about 30 minutes before decorating. Decorate with icings, candies and decors as shown in photo. Use peanut butter sandwich crackers as large train wheels. Assemble train on board or platter. *Makes 1 (4-car) train cookie*

continued on page 56

Choo-Choo Train, continued

Blue Cookie Glaze

2 cups powdered sugar
7 to 9 tablespoons heavy
cream, divided
Liquid or paste food
colorings

1 Combine powdered sugar
and 6 tablespoons cream
in medium bowl; whisk until
smooth. Add enough remaining
cream, 1 tablespoon at a
time, to make a medium-thick
pourable glaze. Tint icing blue
with food coloring, a few drops
at a time, until desired color is
achieved.

Makes 1 cup glaze

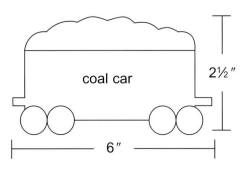

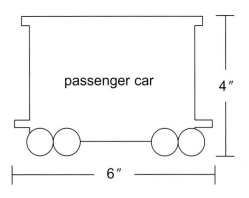

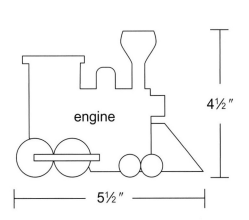

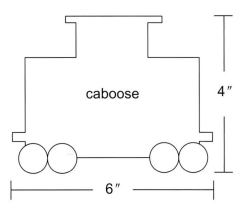

Space Shuttles & Astronauts

What you need:

1 package (about 18 ounces) refrigerated sugar cookie dough
All-purpose flour (optional)

DECORATIONS
Assorted colored frostings, colored glazes, colored gels, colored sugars, small decors and hard candies

SUPPLIES
Cardboard

1 Draw patterns for space shuttle and astronaut on cardboard using the following diagrams; cut out patterns.

2 Preheat oven to 350°F. Grease cookie sheets.

3 Remove dough from wrapper according to package directions. Divide dough into 2 equal sections. Reserve 1 section; cover and refrigerate remaining section.

4 Roll reserved dough on lightly floured surface to ¼-inch thickness. Sprinkle with flour to minimize sticking, if necessary. Lay sheet of waxed paper over dough. Place patterns over waxed paper. Cut dough around patterns with sharp knife; remove patterns and waxed paper. Place cookies 2 inches apart on prepared cookie sheets. Repeat with remaining dough.

5 Bake 10 to 12 minutes or until edges are lightly browned. Remove from oven. Let cool on cookie sheets 2 minutes. Remove to wire racks; cool completely.

6 Decorate cookies with colored frostings, glazes, gels, sugars, decors and hard candies as shown in photo.
Makes 8 cookies

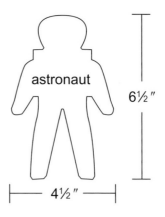

astronaut — 6½" — 4½"

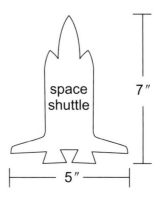

space shuttle — 7" — 5"

Space Shuttle & Astronauts

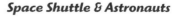

Lollipop Clowns

What you need:

**1 package (about
   18 ounces) refrigerated
   red, green or blue
   cookie dough***
**All-purpose flour
   (optional)**

DECORATIONS
**Assorted colored icings
   and hard candies**

SUPPLIES
18 (4-inch) lollipop sticks

*If colored dough is unavailable,
sugar cookie dough can be tinted
with paste food colorings.

1 Preheat oven to 350°F.

2 Remove dough from
   wrapper according to
package directions. Divide
dough into 2 equal sections.
Reserve 1 section; cover and
refrigerate remaining section.

3 Roll reserved dough on
   lightly floured surface to
⅛-inch thickness. Sprinkle with
flour to minimize sticking, if
necessary.

4 Cut out cookies using
   3½-inch round cookie
cutter. Place lollipop sticks on
cookies so that tips of sticks are
imbedded in cookies. Carefully
turn cookies so sticks are in
back; place on ungreased
cookie sheets.

5 Bake 8 to 10 minutes or
   until firm but not brown.
Let cool on cookie sheets
2 minutes. Remove to wire
racks; cool completely.

6 Decorate cookies with
   icings as shown in photo.
                *Makes about
                1½ dozen cookies*

Tip: *These happy clown faces
      make the perfect topping
for a birthday cake. Stick a Lollipop
Clown, one for each child, in the
cake for a wonderful circus themed
party.*

Surprise Cookies

**1 package (about
 18 ounces) refrigerated
 sugar cookie dough
All-purpose flour
 (optional)**

FILLINGS

**Any combination of
 walnut halves, whole
 almonds, chocolate-
 covered raisins or
 caramel candy squares**

DECORATIONS

Assorted colored sugars

1 Grease cookie sheets.

2 Remove dough from
 wrapper according to
package directions. Divide
dough into 4 equal sections.
Reserve 1 section; cover and
refrigerate remaining 3 sections.

3 Roll reserved dough to
 ¼-inch thickness. Sprinkle
with flour to minimize sticking,
if necessary. Cut out 3-inch
square cookie with sharp knife.
Transfer cookie to prepared
cookie sheet.

4 Place desired "surprise"
 filling in center of cookie.
(If using caramel candy square,
place so that caramel forms
diamond shape within square.)

5 Bring up 4 corners of
 dough towards center;
pinch gently to seal. Repeat
steps with remaining dough and
fillings, placing cookies about
2 inches apart on prepared
cookie sheets. Sprinkle with
colored sugar, if desired.
Freeze cookies 20 minutes.

6 Preheat oven to 350°F.

7 Bake 9 to 11 minutes or
 until edges are lightly
browned. Remove to wire racks;
cool completely.

*Makes about
14 cookies*

Tip: *Make extra batches of
 these simple cookies and
store them in the freezer in heavy
resealable plastic freezer bags.
Take out a few at a time for kids'
after-school treats.*

Cookie Tools

1 package (about 18 ounces) refrigerated chocolate cookie dough*
All-purpose flour (optional)

DECORATIONS
White Decorator Frosting (page 66)
Assorted colored sprinkles and colored frostings

SUPPLIES
Cardboard

*If refrigerated chocolate cookie dough is unavailable, add ¼ cup unsweetened cocoa powder to refrigerated sugar cookie dough. Beat in large bowl at high speed of electric mixer until will blended.

1 Draw patterns for tools on cardboard, using diagrams on page 66; cut out patterns.

2 Preheat oven to 350°F.

3 Remove dough from wrapper according to package directions. Divide dough into 2 equal sections. Reserve 1 section; cover and refrigerate remaining section.

4 Roll reserved dough on lightly floured surface to ⅛-inch thickness. Sprinkle with flour to minimize sticking, if necessary.

5 Lay sheet of waxed paper over dough. Place patterns over waxed paper. Cut dough around patterns with sharp knife; remove patterns and waxed paper. Place cookies 2 inches apart on ungreased cookie sheets. Repeat with remaining dough and any scraps.

6 Bake 8 to 10 minutes or until firm, but not browned. Let cool on cookie sheets 2 minutes. Remove to wire racks; cool completely.

7 Spread frosting evenly over top of each cookie. Decorate with sprinkles and frostings. *Makes about 2 dozen cookies*

continued on page 66

Cookie Tools, continued

White Decorator Frosting

1 pound powdered sugar
½ cup vegetable shortening
or unsalted butter
1 tablespoon corn syrup
6 to 8 tablespoons milk
Assorted paste food
colorings

1 Beat sugar, shortening, corn syrup and milk in medium bowl at high speed of electric mixer 2 minutes or until fluffy. Add food colorings to achieve desired colors.

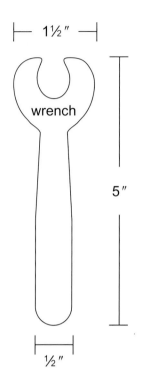

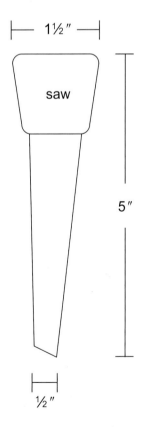

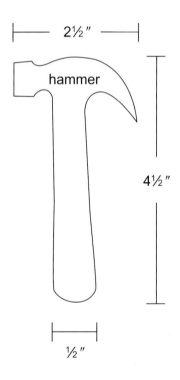

"Radical" Peanut Butter Pizza Cookies

COOKIES

 1 Butter Flavor* CRISCO®
   Stick or 1 cup Butter
   Flavor CRISCO®
   all-vegetable shortening
1¼ cups granulated sugar,
   divided
 1 cup packed dark brown
   sugar
 1 cup creamy peanut butter
 2 eggs
 1 teaspoon baking soda
 1 teaspoon vanilla
 ½ teaspoon salt
 2 cups all-purpose flour
 2 cups quick oats,
   uncooked

PIZZA SAUCE

 2 cups milk chocolate chips
 ¼ Butter Flavor* CRISCO®
   Stick or ¼ cup Butter
   Flavor CRISCO®
   all-vegetable shortening

PIZZA TOPPINGS (page 68)

DRIZZLE

 1 cup chopped white
   confectionery coating

*Butter Flavor Crisco is artificially flavored.

1 Heat oven to 350°F.
Place sheets of foil on
countertop for cooling cookies.

2 For cookies, combine
1 cup shortening, 1 cup
granulated sugar and brown
sugar in large bowl. Beat at low
speed of electric mixer until well
blended. Add peanut butter,
eggs, baking soda, vanilla and
salt. Mix about 2 minutes or until
well blended. Stir in flour and
oats with spoon.

3 Place remaining ¼ cup
granulated sugar in small
bowl.

4 Measure ¼ cup dough.
Shape into ball. Repeat
with remaining dough. Roll each
ball in sugar. Place 4 inches
apart on ungreased cookie
sheets. Flatten into 4-inch
circles.

5 Bake at 350°F for 8 to 10
minutes. *Do not overbake.*
Use back of spoon to flatten
center and up to edge of each
hot cookie to resemble pizza
crust. Cool 5 to 8 minutes on
baking sheet. Remove pizza to
foil to cool completely.

6 For pizza sauce, combine
chocolate chips and ¼ cup
shortening in large microwave-
safe measuring cup or bowl.

continued on page 68

"Radical" Peanut Butter Pizza Cookies, continued

Microwave at MEDIUM (50%) 2 to 3 minutes or until chips are shiny and soft (or melt on rangetop in small saucepan on very low heat). Stir until smooth. Spoon 2 teaspoons melted chocolate into center of each cookie. Spread to inside edge. Sprinkle desired toppings over chocolate.

7 For drizzle, place chopped confectionery coating in heavy resealable plastic food storage bag. Seal. Microwave at MEDIUM (50%). Knead bag after 1 minute. Repeat until smooth (or melt by placing in bowl of hot water). Cut pinpoint hole in corner of bag. Squeeze out and drizzle over cookies.

Makes about 2 dozen cookies

PIZZA TOPPINGS
Mmmmm: candy coated chocolate pieces
Beary good: gummy bears
Jumbo jewels: small pieces of gumdrops
Bubble gum-like: round sprinkles and balls
German chocolate: chopped pecans and flake coconut
Cherries jubilee: candied cherries and slivered almonds

Rocky road: miniature marshmallows and mini semisweet chocolate chips
Harvest mix: candy corn and chopped peanuts
Ants and logs: cashews and raisins

Tip: These cookies are a great project for kids' parties and rainy days. Bake the cookies ahead of time and let the children create their own cookie pizzas.

"Radical" Peanut Butter Pizza Cookies

CREATIVE COOKIE CENTER

Moons and Stars

What you need:

1 cup (2 sticks) butter,
   softened
1 cup sugar
1 egg
2 teaspoons lemon peel
½ teaspoon almond extract
3 cups all-purpose flour
½ cup ground almonds
   All-purpose flour
   (optional)

DECORATIONS

   Assorted colored icings,
   hard candies and
   colored sprinkles

1 Preheat oven to 350°F. Grease cookie sheets. Beat butter, sugar, egg, lemon peel and almond extract in large bowl at medium speed of electric mixer until fluffy.

2 Combine flour and almonds in medium bowl. Add to butter mixture; mix only to incorporate flour.

3 Roll dough on lightly floured surface to ¼-inch thickness. Cut out cookies using cookie cutters. Place 2 inches apart on cookie sheets.

4 Bake 7 to 9 minutes or until set. Cool on cookie sheets 2 minutes. Remove to wire racks; cool completely. Decorate. *Makes about 4 dozen cookies*

70

Crayon Cookies

1 cup (2 sticks) butter, softened
2 teaspoons vanilla
½ cup powdered sugar
2¼ cups all-purpose flour
¼ teaspoon salt
Assorted paste food colorings

DECORATIONS
1½ cups chocolate chips
1½ teaspoons shortening

1 Preheat oven to 350°F. Grease cookie sheets.

2 Beat butter and vanilla in large bowl at high speed of electric mixer until fluffy. Add sugar; beat at medium speed until blended. Combine flour and salt in small bowl. Gradually add to butter mixture.

3 Divide dough into 10 equal sections. Reserve 1 section; cover and refrigerate remaining 9 sections. Combine reserved section and desired food coloring in small bowl; blend well.

4 Cut dough into 2 equal sections. Roll each section into 5-inch log. Pinch one end to resemble crayon tip. Place cookies 2 inches apart on prepared cookie sheets. Repeat with remaining 9 sections of dough and desired food colorings.

5 Bake 15 to 18 minutes or until edges are lightly browned. Cool completely on cookie sheets.

6 Combine chocolate chips and shortening in small microwavable bowl. Microwave on HIGH 1 to 1½ minutes, stirring after 1 minute, or until smooth. Decorate with chocolate mixture as shown in photo.
Makes 20 cookies

Lady Bugs

¾ **cup shortening**
½ **cup sugar**
¼ **cup honey**
1 **egg**
½ **teaspoon vanilla**
2 **cups all-purpose flour**
⅓ **cup cornmeal**
1 **teaspoon baking powder**
½ **teaspoon salt**

DECORATIONS
Orange and black icings and yellow candy-coated pieces

1 Beat shortening, sugar and honey in large bowl at medium speed of electric mixer until light and fluffy. Add egg and vanilla; mix until well blended.

2 Combine flour, cornmeal, baking powder and salt in medium bowl. Add to shortening mixture; mix at low speed until blended. Cover; refrigerate several hours or overnight, if desired.

3 Preheat oven to 375°F.

4 Divide dough into 24 equal sections. Shape each section into 2×1¼-inch oval-shaped ball. Place balls 2 inches apart on ungreased cookie sheets.

5 Bake 10 to 12 minutes or until lightly browned. Cool on cookie sheets 2 minutes. Remove to wire racks; cool completely.

6 Decorate cookies with icings and candies as shown in photo.
Makes 2 dozen cookies

Rollerblade Cookies

What you need:

1¼ cups honey
1 cup packed brown sugar
½ cup (1 stick) butter, softened
1 egg yolk
5½ cups self-rising flour
1 teaspoon ground ginger
1 teaspoon ground cinnamon
½ cup milk
1 egg white
1 tablespoon cold water

DECORATIONS

Toasted oats cereal
Assorted colored decorating icings, sugars and sprinkles

1 Beat honey, sugar, butter and egg yolk in large bowl at medium speed of electric mixer until light and fluffy.

2 Combine flour, ginger and cinnamon in small bowl. Add alternately with milk to butter mixture; beat just until combined. Cover; refrigerate 30 minutes.

3 Preheat oven to 350°F. Grease cookie sheets.

4 Roll dough on lightly floured surface to ¼-inch thickness. Cut out cookies using 3½-inch boot cookie cutter or pattern (see page 5). Place 2 inches apart on prepared cookie sheets.

5 Beat egg white and water in small bowl until combined. Lightly brush bottom of each boot with egg white mixture. Place 6 toasted oats on bottom of each boot to represent wheels.

6 Bake 8 to 10 minutes or until lightly browned. Cool 2 minutes on cookie sheets. Remove to wire racks; cool completely.

7 Decorate cookies with colored icings, sugars and sprinkles as shown in photo.

*Makes about
4 dozen cookies*

Sunflower Cookies in Flowerpots

Butter Cookie Dough
(page 80)
1 container (16 ounces)
vanilla frosting
Yellow food coloring
Powdered sugar
1 gallon ice cream (any
flavor), softened
Brown decorating icing
24 chocolate sandwich
cookies, crushed
1 cup shredded coconut,
tinted green*

SUPPLIES
12 (6-inch) lollipop sticks
6 plastic drinking straws
12 (6½-ounce) paper cups
Pastry bag and small
writing tip
12 new (3¼-inch-diameter)
ceramic flowerpots,
about 3½ inches tall

*See Tinting Coconut, page 5.

1 Preheat oven to 350°F.
Grease cookie sheets.

2 Prepare Butter Cookie
dough. Roll dough on
lightly-floured surface to ⅛-inch
thickness. Cut out cookies with
fluted cookie cutter; place on
prepared cookie sheets.

3 Bake 8 to 10 minutes or
until edges are lightly
browned. Remove to wire racks;
cool completely.

4 Color vanilla frosting
with yellow food coloring.
Measure out ⅔ cup colored
frosting; cover and set aside
remaining frosting. Blend
enough additional powdered
sugar into measured ⅔ cup
frosting to make very thick
frosting. Use about 1 tablespoon
thickened frosting to attach
lollipop stick to back of each
cookie. Set aside to allow
frosting to dry completely.

5 Cut straws crosswise in
half. Hold 1 straw upright
in center of each cup; pack ice
cream around straw, completely
filling each cup with ice cream.
(Be sure straw sticks up out of
ice cream.) Freeze until ice
cream is hardened, 3 to 4 hours.

continued on page 80

*Sunflower Cookies
in Flowerpots*

Sunflower Cookies in Flowerpots, continued

6 Frost front side of each cookie as desired with remaining frosting. Spoon brown icing into pastry bag fitted with writing tip; use to decorate cookies as shown in photo.

7 To serve, place cups filled with ice cream in flowerpots. Top with cookie crumbs to resemble dirt. Sprinkle tinted coconut around straw to resemble grass. Clip straw off to make it even with ice cream, taking care not to fill straw with crumbs or coconut. Insert lollipop stick, with cookie attached, into opening in each straw to stand cookie upright in flowerpot.

Makes 12 servings

Butter Cookie Dough
¾ cup butter, softened
¼ cup granulated sugar
¼ cup packed light brown
     sugar
1 egg yolk
1¾ cups all-purpose flour
¾ teaspoon baking powder
⅛ teaspoon salt

1 Combine butter, granulated sugar, brown sugar and egg yolk in medium bowl. Add flour, baking powder and salt; mix well.

2 Cover; refrigerate about 4 hours or until firm.

Tip: To create a summer flower cookie garden, pair these Sunflower Cookies in Flowerpots with a batch of Lady Bugs (page 74) and beautiful Butterfly Cookies (page 84).

Chocolate Lattice Cookie Baskets

What you need:

¾ cup sugar
½ cup (1 stick) butter, softened
1 egg
1 teaspoon vanilla
2½ cups all-purpose flour
½ cup unsweetened cocoa powder
½ teaspoon baking powder
¼ teaspoon salt
½ cup sour cream

DECORATIONS

Brown Royal Icing (page 82)
4 red licorice twists
Assorted candies

1. Beat sugar and butter in large bowl at high speed of electric mixer until light and fluffy. Add egg and vanilla; mix until blended.

2. Combine flour, cocoa, baking powder and salt in medium bowl. Add half flour mixture to butter mixture; mix at low speed until well blended. Add sour cream; mix well. Add remaining flour mixture; mix well. Divide dough into 2 equal sections. Cover and refrigerate several hours or overnight.

3. Roll 1 section of dough on well-floured surface to ¼-inch thickness. Transfer to parchment-lined cookie sheet. Cut dough into 8×7-inch rectangle. Reserve scraps. With 8-inch side facing you, cut lengthwise into 8×5-inch piece and 8×2-inch piece. Place pieces horizontally with larger piece above smaller piece.

4. Leaving ½-inch uncut border at top edge of 8×5-inch piece, vertically cut into 16 (½-inch-wide) equal strips. Cut 8×2-inch piece horizontally into 4 (½-inch-wide) equal strips. Cover and refrigerate 10 minutes.

5. Place 8×5-inch piece with strips facing you vertically. Beginning on your left, fold every other strip back and over the top border.

6. Place 1 strip from 8×2-inch piece horizontally across unfolded strips. Unfold strips back to their original position.

7. Beginning with the second vertical strip on your left, fold every other strip back. Insert another horizontal strip as directed in step 6. Repeat with remaining 2 horizontal strips.

continued on page 82

Chocolate Lattice Cookie Baskets, continued

8 Cut off ½-inch top border. Flatten lattice slightly with palm of hand. Straighten edges with spatula so lattice measures 8×4 inches, if necessary. Chill 10 minutes.

9 Preheat oven to 350°F.

10 Cut lattice into eight 2-inch squares. Roll reserved scraps on lightly floured surface to ¼-inch thickness. Cut two 2¼-inch squares. Place on cookie sheet with lattice.

11 Bake 15 to 17 minutes or until set. Cool completely on cookie sheet set on wire rack. Repeat steps 3 through 11 with remaining dough.

12 Place icing in small resealable plastic food storage bag; cut off small corner of bag.

13 Lightly grease parchment or waxed paper cut to fit large cookie sheet or tray. Place one 2¼-inch-square basket bottom on parchment paper. Pipe icing on edges of 3 sides of lattice squares. Position lattice squares to form 4 sided box, leaving plain sides at top.

Place small cups against outer sides to hold in place until set. Pipe a small amount of icing to ends of 1 licorice twist. Press licorice ends into opposite basket seams to create a handle. Let stand at least 4 hours before filling. Repeat steps with remaining cookie basket pieces.

Makes 4 baskets

Brown Royal Icing

1 egg white, at room temperature
2 to 2½ cups sifted powdered sugar
½ teaspoon almond extract
Assorted liquid or paste food colorings

1 Beat egg white in small bowl at high speed of electric mixer until foamy.

2 Gradually add 2 cups powdered sugar and almond extract. Beat at low speed until moistened. Increase speed to high and beat until icing is stiff, adding additional powdered sugar if needed. Tint with food colorings until a shade of brown that matches lattice dough is achieved.

Chocolate Lattice Cookie Baskets

Butterfly Cookies

What you need:

2¼ cups all-purpose flour
¼ teaspoon salt
1 cup sugar
¾ cup (1½ sticks) butter, softened
1 egg
1 teaspoon vanilla
1 teaspoon almond extract

DECORATIONS

White frosting, assorted food colorings, colored sugars, assorted small decors, gummy fruit and hard candies

1 Combine flour and salt in medium bowl; set aside.

2 Beat sugar and butter in large bowl at medium speed of electric mixer until fluffy. Beat in egg, vanilla and almond extract. Gradually add flour mixture. Beat at low speed until well blended.

3 Divide dough into 2 equal sections. Cover; refrigerate 30 minutes or until firm.

4 Preheat oven to 350°F. Grease cookie sheets.

5 Reserve 1 section; cover and refrigerate remaining section. Roll reserved dough on lightly floured surface to ¼-inch thickness. Cut out cookies using butterfly cookie cutters. Place cutouts on prepared cookie sheets. Repeat with remaining dough.

6 Bake 12 to 15 minutes or until edges are lightly browned. Remove to wire racks; cool completely.

7 Tint portions of white frosting with assorted food colorings. Spread desired color of frosting over cookie. Repeat with remaining cookies.

8 Decorate with colored sugars, assorted small decors, gummy fruit and hard candies as desired.

*Makes about
20 to 22 cookies*

Checkerboard Cookie

1 cup sugar
¾ cup (1½ sticks) butter,
   softened
2 eggs
1 teaspoon vanilla
2¾ cups self-rising flour
   All-purpose flour

DECORATIONS
   Red and black decorating
   icings

1 Beat sugar and butter in large bowl at high speed of electric mixer until light and fluffy. Add eggs and vanilla; beat until well blended. Add self-rising flour; stir until just combined. Cover and refrigerate 30 minutes.

2 Preheat oven to 350°F. Grease cookie sheets.

3 Roll ¼ of dough on lightly floured surface to ¼-inch thickness. Cut 24 circles with 1-inch round cookie cutter. Place on prepared cookie sheets.

4 Bake 8 to 10 minutes or until cookies turn light golden brown. Cool on cookie sheets 2 minutes. Remove to wire racks; cool completely.

5 Combine scraps of dough with remaining dough. Roll on lightly floured surface to 12-inch square. Place on greased 15½×12-inch cookie sheet.

6 Bake 10 to 12 minutes or until middle does not leave indentation when lightly touched with fingertips. Cool on cookie sheet 5 minutes. Slide checkerboard onto wire rack; cool completely.

7 Divide surface of checkerboard into 8 equal rows containing 8 equal columns. Alternate every other square with red and black icing to create checkerboard. Spread red icing on 12 checker playing pieces and black on remaining 12 checker playing pieces. Allow pieces to stand until icing is set. Place red pieces on black squares and black pieces on red squares.

Makes 1 checkerboard cookie

Peanut Butter Bears

What you need:

1 cup SKIPPY® Creamy Peanut Butter
1 cup (2 sticks) MAZOLA® Margarine or butter, softened
1 cup packed brown sugar
⅔ cup KARO® Light or Dark Corn Syrup
2 eggs
4 cups flour, divided
1 tablespoon baking powder
1 teaspoon cinnamon (optional)
¼ teaspoon salt

1 In large bowl with mixer at medium speed, beat peanut butter, margarine, brown sugar, corn syrup and eggs until smooth. Reduce speed; beat in 2 cups of flour, baking powder, cinnamon and salt. With spoon, stir in remaining 2 cups flour. Wrap dough in plastic wrap; refrigerate 2 hours.

2 Preheat oven to 325°F. Divide dough in half; set aside half.

3 On floured surface roll out half the dough to ⅛-inch thickness. Cut with floured bear cookie cutter. Repeat with remaining dough.

4 Use scraps of dough to make bear faces. Make one small ball of dough for muzzle. Form 3 smaller balls of dough and press gently to create eyes and nose; bake as directed.

5 Bake bears on ungreased cookie sheets 10 minutes or until lightly browned. Remove from cookie sheets; cool completely on wire racks. Decorate as desired, using frosting to create paws, ears and bow ties.   *Makes about 3 dozen bears*

Baseball Caps

What you need:

**1 cup (2 sticks) butter,
   softened
7 ounces almond paste
¾ cup sugar
1 egg
1 teaspoon vanilla
¼ teaspoon salt
3 cups all-purpose flour**

DECORATIONS
**Assorted colored icings
and colored candies**

1 Preheat oven to 350°F.
Grease cookie sheets.

2 Beat butter, almond paste,
sugar, egg, vanilla and salt
in large bowl at high speed of
electric mixer until light and
fluffy. Add flour all at once; stir
just to combine.

3 Roll ¼ of dough on lightly
floured surface to ⅛-inch
thickness. Cut out 1-inch
circles. Place circles 2 inches
apart on prepared cookie
sheets.

4 Roll remaining dough into
1-inch balls. Place one
ball on top of half dough circle
so about ½ inch of circle sticks
out to form bill of baseball cap.

5 Bake 10 to 12 minutes or
until lightly browned. If
bills brown too quickly, cut small
strips of foil and cover with
shiny side of foil facing you.
Cool on cookie sheets 2 minutes.
Remove to wire racks; cool
completely.

6 Decorate with icings and
candies as shown in photo.
*Makes about
3 dozen cookies*

Tip: *Using a 1-tablespoon
scoop is a great way to
keep the baseball caps uniform in
size and professional looking.*

Burger Bliss

BUNS

1 package (about 18 ounces) refrigerated sugar cookie dough
½ cup creamy peanut butter
⅓ cup all-purpose flour
¼ cup packed brown sugar
½ teaspoon vanilla
Beaten egg white and sesame seeds (optional)

BURGERS

½ (18-ounce) package refrigerated sugar cookie dough*
3 tablespoons unsweetened cocoa powder
2 tablespoons packed brown sugar
½ teaspoon vanilla
Red, yellow and green decorating icings

*Reserve remaining dough for another use.

1 Preheat oven to 350°F. Grease cookie sheets. For buns, remove dough from wrapper according to package directions; place in large bowl. Let dough stand at room temperature about 15 minutes.

2 Add peanut butter, flour, brown sugar and vanilla to dough in bowl; beat at medium speed of electric mixer until well blended. Shape into 48 (1-inch) balls; place 2 inches apart on prepared cookie sheets.

3 Bake 14 minutes or until lightly browned. If desired, remove cookies from oven after 10 minutes; brush half of cookies with egg white and sprinkle with sesame seeds, if desired. Return to oven 4 minutes to finish baking and brown sesame seeds. Remove from oven. Cool on cookie sheets 2 to 3 minutes. Remove to wire racks; cool completely.

4 For burgers, remove ½ package of dough from wrapper according to package directions. Beat dough, cocoa, brown sugar and vanilla in large bowl at medium speed of electric mixer until well blended. Shape into 24 (1-inch) balls; place 2 inches apart on prepared cookie sheets. Flatten cookies with tines of fork to a ¼-inch thickness with a diameter slightly larger than buns.

5 Bake 12 minutes or until firm. Cool on cookie sheets 2 to 3 minutes. Remove to wire racks; cool completely.

6 To assemble, use icing to attach burgers to flat sides of 24 buns; pipe red, yellow and green icings on burgers. Top with remaining buns.

Makes 2 dozen sandwich cookies

ACKNOWLEDGMENTS

*The publisher would like to thank the companies and organizations
listed below for the use of their recipes and photographs
in this publication.*

Best Foods

Hershey Foods Corporation

M&M/MARS

The Procter & Gamble Company

METRIC CONVERSION CHART

VOLUME MEASUREMENTS (dry)

$\frac{1}{8}$ teaspoon = 0.5 mL
$\frac{1}{4}$ teaspoon = 1 mL
$\frac{1}{2}$ teaspoon = 2 mL
$\frac{3}{4}$ teaspoon = 4 mL
1 teaspoon = 5 mL
1 tablespoon = 15 mL
2 tablespoons = 30 mL
$\frac{1}{4}$ cup = 60 mL
$\frac{1}{3}$ cup = 75 mL
$\frac{1}{2}$ cup = 125 mL
$\frac{2}{3}$ cup = 150 mL
$\frac{3}{4}$ cup = 175 mL
1 cup = 250 mL
2 cups = 1 pint = 500 mL
3 cups = 750 mL
4 cups = 1 quart = 1 L

VOLUME MEASUREMENTS (fluid)

1 fluid ounce (2 tablespoons) = 30 mL
4 fluid ounces ($\frac{1}{2}$ cup) = 125 mL
8 fluid ounces (1 cup) = 250 mL
12 fluid ounces (1$\frac{1}{2}$ cups) = 375 mL
16 fluid ounces (2 cups) = 500 mL

WEIGHTS (mass)

$\frac{1}{2}$ ounce = 15 g
1 ounce = 30 g
3 ounces = 90 g
4 ounces = 120 g
8 ounces = 225 g
10 ounces = 285 g
12 ounces = 360 g
16 ounces = 1 pound = 450 g

DIMENSIONS

$\frac{1}{16}$ inch = 2 mm
$\frac{1}{8}$ inch = 3 mm
$\frac{1}{4}$ inch = 6 mm
$\frac{1}{2}$ inch = 1.5 cm
$\frac{3}{4}$ inch = 2 cm
1 inch = 2.5 cm

OVEN TEMPERATURES

250°F = 120°C
275°F = 140°C
300°F = 150°C
325°F = 160°C
350°F = 180°C
375°F = 190°C
400°F = 200°C
425°F = 220°C
450°F = 230°C

BAKING PAN SIZES

Utensil	Size in Inches/Quarts	Metric Volume	Size in Centimeters
Baking or Cake Pan (square or rectangular)	8×8×2	2 L	20×20×5
	9×9×2	2.5 L	23×23×5
	12×8×2	3 L	30×20×5
	13×9×2	3.5 L	33×23×5
Loaf Pan	8×4×3	1.5 L	20×10×7
	9×5×3	2 L	23×13×7
Round Layer Cake Pan	8×1½	1.2 L	20×4
	9×1½	1.5 L	23×4
Pie Plate	8×1¼	750 mL	20×3
	9×1¼	1 L	23×3
Baking Dish or Casserole	1 quart	1 L	—
	1½ quart	1.5 L	—
	2 quart	2 L	—